The Ann Arbor Guide

to

Special Educational Needs

Dr Martin Phillips DSc. PhD
Dr Mary Ann Phillips D.Ed.

The Ann Arbor Guide to Special Educational Needs
© Ann Arbor Publishers Limited

First published 2005
ISBN 1 900506 17 3

Typeset and design by The Design Desk, Main Road, Milfield, Wooler,
Northumberland, NE71 6JD. www.thedesigndesk.co.uk

Front cover design was inspired by research at Cambridge University which determined that
word recognition relies on the first and last letter being in the correct place.

This book has been designed using a large font size and clear print layout to aid sight
impaired readers.

The authors gratefully acknowledge the individuals and organisations who have contributed
to this book.

Published by: Ann Arbor Publishers Limited, P.O.Box 1, Belford,
Northumberland, NE70 7JX. www.annarbor.co.uk

CONTENTS

The Ann Arbor Guide to Special Educational Needs contains ten sections, each explaining, in lay terms, some of the most common difficulties and disabilities suffered by some children and which, if not identified and helped, may follow them into adulthood.

Some of these disabilities are included in the Special Educational Needs Disability Act (SENDA – 2002) but all should be within the remit of the Special Educational Needs Co-ordinator (SENCO).

This Guide should be read in conjunction with the current Ann Arbor catalogue* as, at the end of each section, the authors direct the parent or non-specialist teacher to the appropriate diagnostic or remediation material and resources available direct from Ann Arbor Publishers – the UK's foremost publishing company for special needs resources. Material can also be ordered on-line at their website which is www.annarbor.co.uk

For further and more detailed explanations of the various disabilities covered in the Guide, parents are directed to relevant websites on the internet.

The authors are an Educational Psychologist / Lecturer and a Specialist Teacher/Lecturer both of whom practise in the UK and the Middle East. They have used the wide range of Ann Arbor materials extensively for over forty years and are Special Education Consultants to the Publishers.

* All Ann Arbor materials listed will be found in the Index of the current Catalogue

Specific Learning Difficulties - Dyslexia

For many years teachers have observed a mysterious anomaly in the classroom. Some children of evident intelligence never learn to read, write or compute at levels commensurate with their ability. Conscientious teachers and parents have realised that many of these *failures* are not due to laziness, especially since many of the affected children are amongst the most industrious in the class. Nor do their difficulties appear to result from stupidity since these particular illiterate children usually exhibit brightness in oral language fluency.

Many parents have been bewildered by the fact that their child has failed to master basic literacy and numeracy skills despite being generally articulate and apparently intelligent in the home environment.

Some of these children have come to be known as dyslexic or suffering from specific learning difficulties.

In 1968 the World Federation of Neurologists met under their Chairman, Dr. Macdonald Critchley, and defined dyslexia as, "A condition in which a person of adequate intelligence fails to master skills of reading and spelling despite motivation, adequate hearing and vision and good socio-economic conditions." Since this time others have attempted a definition of dyslexia which is both accurate and acceptable. Perhaps the most useful is that given by Dr. Harry Chasty, former Director of Studies at the Dyslexia Institute. He said, "A dyslexic is a person with a different and less efficient form of neurological organisation for language." Many other professionals have attempted to define this educational deficiency. In 1932 Dr. Samuel Orton, an American neurologist, coined the term *Strephosymbolia* which he defined literally as twisted symbols. He was attempting to classify the children who perceived letters inverted, backwards or in a distorted fashion. Later another term appeared, *Alexia* which defines the mysterious inability of intelligent people to recognise the printed word. Alexia is still used by many professionals in many fields. The word *dyslexia* was first used in 1887 by Professor Berlin of Stuttgart University but over the years terms like *word blindness, legasthenia, amblyopia* and *typholexia* have amazed laymen and confused the professionals. In addition, *dysgraphia* is a term which has been used for disorders in handwriting and *dyscalculia* for faulty arithmetic perception. Each of these terms has a useful meaning but none has aroused so much controversy as the word *dyslexia*.

Many critics of the term dyslexia argue that its existence was unknown until the post-war period. The facts, however, prove otherwise. Prior to 1870 only a privileged few had the opportunity to study and even after the introduction of compulsory schooling for all, large classes and unqualified teachers did little for the standards of literacy. In 1896 Pringle Morgan, a general practitioner from Seaford, used the term "word blindness" to describe the case of a fourteen-year-old intelligent non-reader at a local preparatory school. Only a few weeks previously James Kerr, Medical Officer of Health for Bradford, had written ". . . but besides the generally dull there are the mentally exceptional, many quite suitable for ordinary schools provided the teacher knows their peculiarities. Almost unique cases are found with most bizarre defects. Agraphia, for instance, may be unintelligible to a teacher, especially if it occurs, as in one of my cases, in a boy who can do arithmetic well so long as it involves Arabic numerals only, but writes gibberish in a neat hand for dictation exercise. A boy with word blindness who can spell the separate letters, is a trouble . . .".

During this time many thought that reading and spelling failure was due to defective brain functioning but already controversy had started over the reasons. Outside Great Britain the syndrome became recognised and early reports came from Holland (1903), Buenos Aires (1903), Germany (1903) and America. Burt (1937) and Schonell (1942) drew attention to poor reading standards, but neither supported the arguments of congenital cerebral deficiency and instead suggested "unfavourable factors in the child and home".

In 1935 in Denmark the Word Blind Institute was founded in Copenhagen by Edith Norrie. Edith Norrie was herself dyslexic and established a special centre for diagnosis and assessment. In Denmark today adequate provision is made for the dyslexic child within the State System and most State schools have their own *Word Blind Class.* If, after studying in this special class for two years, the child is still under-achieving, arrangements are made for the child to be sent to the Institute in Copenhagen on a full-time basis for an intensive teaching programme which lasts for two years. All fees are paid by the State and the teachers at the Institute have previously undergone a special post-graduate training for which they receive an additional diploma.

The Education Act (1944) required local authorities to provide special schools for the education of the physically and mentally handicapped and to make special provision within ordinary schools for the education of children seriously retarded in literacy. Too few teachers and educational psychologists were able to put this policy into effect.

In 1953 the National Foundation for Educational Research in England and Wales (NFER) published a report on a survey of seven-year-old children and this found that 45 per cent had not mastered the mechanics of language and of this 45 per cent, 19 per cent were not reading at all. These figures brought renewed interest in old theories of word blindness or dyslexia and teaching methods came under review.

In England in 1962 the Invalid Children's Aid Association (ICAA) established the Word Blind Association for the study of dyslexia and during the next decade a number of organisations sprang up to enquire into the problems of the dyslexic child.

In 1972 the North Surrey Dyslexic Society found that public awareness of dyslexia led to an unsatisfied demand for treatment. They established the Dyslexia Institute which now provides dyslexics with an advisory service, professional assessment and specialised teaching. As well as other dyslexia organizations, universities and colleges, it also trains specialist teachers and undertakes research into the causes of dyslexia.

Also in 1972 the Tizzard report was published. This Government report found that the term dyslexia was "unhelpful" and recommended that specific reading retardation was a more appropriate term. The report did, however, recommend general screening arrangements to locate retarded readers.

Despite the Government's education policy statement in the Queen's Speech (1974) that it would continue to give priority to areas of greatest need and to children with specific difficulties, the Department of Education and Science still did not recognise dyslexia as a statutory category of handicap. In 1970 however, the Chronically Sick and Disabled Persons Act included dyslexia as an educational disability for which local education authorities are empowered to provide special education, but there was no compulsion upon them to do so. In 1975 the Bullock report stated that 10 per cent of children were backward readers and the National Association for Remedial Education gave evidence to the Warnock Committee suggesting that 15 per cent would be the minimum number of children likely to require help. Of this 15 per cent only 2 per cent were in special schools leaving 13 per cent in the normal school system in need of specialist help. Statistics recently published state that one in ten children leave school with a reading age below nine years, producing a total of 70,000-90,000 "illiterate" school leavers annually (Widlake). A survey by the Dyslexia Institute has shown that at least 32,000 children enter our schools each year handicapped by dyslexia and that their disappointing scholastic performance is still often attributed to laziness, stupidity or a disturbed background.

The 1993 Education Act placed a duty on the Secretary of State to issue a Code of Practice on Special Educational Needs. The first Code was published in 1994 and placed statutory obligations on Local Education Authorities in England, Wales and N.Ireland (not Scotland), to identify and make appropriate provision for those children with special educational needs. Specific Learning Difficulties was included in the Code.

The Code of Practice also gave LEA's the power to issue a Statement of Special Educational Needs and gave parents the right of Appeal to an independent Special Educational Needs Tribunal if they did not agree with the LEA's decisions.

The Code of Practice was revised in 2002. Amongst the new provisions was a greater right for children with SEN to be educated in main-stream schools and greater emphasis on working partnerships between parents and LEA's.

Finally, the Special Educational Needs and Disability Act 2001 prohibits schools, colleges and universities from treating disabled pupils less favourably for a reason relating to their disability and they must make "reasonable adjustment" to ensure this. Severe Dyslexia is classified as a disability under the terms of the Act.

Controversy over terminology often serves as a stumbling block for eliciting any practical application of research. Money (1962) wrote, "It is not at all rare in psychological medicine nor in other branches of medicine that a disease should have no unique identifying sign, that uniqueness being in the pattern of signs that appear in contiguity. Out of context each sign might also be encountered in other diseases, or in different intensities, in the healthy. Specific dyslexia is no exception to this rule."

In traditional classroom teaching methods it is assumed that all children can readily master three kinds of language symbol. Oral/aural used in talking and hearing, the printed symbol used in reading and the written symbol used in handwriting. It is also assumed that children are capable of progressing automatically from left to right across the page, and from top to bottom down the page. For perhaps 10 per cent of the school population these basic assumptions about learning to read are not valid. Many dyslexic children do not master language symbols and cannot perceive left to right and top to bottom. To interpret a symbol, a child must see and interpret, hear the sound, interpret its meaning and say it, and then feel the hand, wrist and arm movement as he writes it. These inter-actions must be simultaneous. If there is a weakness in any one of these perceptual pathways, some form of dyslexia is the result.

The dyslexic child with a visual perceptual handicap has a basic inability to translate printed language symbols into meaning. This inability has nothing to do with visual acuity (the ability to see) but the impairment is due to the information received by the eye being incorrectly processed by the brain. The child with an auditory perceptual handicap has been likened to the person who has tone-deafness towards music. Because the child cannot discriminate between small differences in vowel or consonant symbols, he is unable to associate specific sounds with their printed symbols.

Another frequently occurring set of symptoms is found in the dysgraphic child. Such a child tends to write using large broken letter forms. As with other kinds of dyslexia, dysgraphic children cannot cope with pressure and speed.

Early recognition of the dyslexic child is of vital importance if effective specialist help is to be given soon enough and parents and teachers should be aware of the set of symptoms which can constitute dyslexia. Some of these are as follows:

- Discrepancy between apparent intelligence and performance at reading and/or spelling.
- Bizarre spelling.
- Confusion between b and d (other letters may be reversed or inverted).
- Difficulty over distinguishing left and right
- Poor short term memory.
- Difficulty over repeating long words.
- Difficulty over repeating numbers – especially in reverse order.
- Difficulty memorising multiplication tables.
- Difficulty remembering months of the year and other common sequences.
- History of clumsiness, late walking, talking, etc.
- Difficulties with pregnancy or at birth.
- Family history of similar learning difficulties.

If a child over eight years possesses three or more of the above set of symptoms it is possible that he or she is dyslexic.

Some advice when dealing with dyslexic children

1.   Don't simply brand him as lazy or careless.
2.   Don't make invidious comparisons with others in his class or family.
3.   Don't put pressure on him in such a way that he becomes frightened of failing or letting you down.
4.   Don't, without his consent, expect him to read aloud to others.
5.   Don't expect him to learn the spelling of a word by writing it out a few times in the hope that it will be remembered - it almost certainly won't.
6.   Don't be surprised if his performance in class is erratic.
7.   Don't be surprised if he tires easily or lacks concentration.
8.   Don't expect him to be able to master a foreign language! The learning of French for example, particularly in a bi-lingual family, frequently confuses the child thus impeding his progress in spelling and reading. The child's level of competency in French is usually abysmally low.
9.   Do encourage him in the things he can do well.
10.   Do express appreciation of effort.
11.   Do read aloud to the dyslexic child.
12.   Do discuss frankly the things that he finds difficult.
13.   Do encourage him to look at words in detail, a few letters at a time.
14.   Do provide structure at home and at school.

Specialist teaching

Since no two dyslexics display the same difficulties, so also, no two dyslexic children can be taught in exactly the same way. For those who have severe perceptual weaknesses it is essential that a structured cumulative and multi-sensory teaching technique is adopted. The children should, whenever possible, be taught in a one-to-one situation by a teacher qualified and experienced in multi-sensory techniques.

Specialist help should be given a little and often and, since many of these children have a limited concentration span, lessons which exceed 20 minutes of actual instruction tend to be counter-productive. Constant reinforcement is necessary. Children with visual perceptual weaknesses will have difficulty in sequencing letters, the days of the week and other common sequences. They may reverse or invert letters and they may see parts of words in reverse. This difficulty in handling information in sequence may also extend to basic arithmetic. Learning to add, subtract, multiply and divide involves frequent changes of direction which contradict the left to right and top to bottom orientation stressed in reading and writing. These children have a tendency to compensate for their perceptual weakness by sub-vocalising (virtually reading aloud to themselves) when attempting to read, a habit which is frequently discouraged by many teachers who are unaware of the child's difficulties.

The child with an auditory perceptual weakness is at a serious disadvantage in standardised tests which involve careful listening, accurate interpretation and quick gestalt formation of what is heard. Time limits on work assignments are the major enemy of the dyslexic child. The most successful methods of specialist treatment seem, at the moment, to be those employing multi-sensory experience. Of these programmes available three are perhaps the most widely used. These are:

* Alpha to Omega by Hornsby and Shear (Heinemann)
* The Dyslexia Institute Literacy programme (only available to D.I.)
* Toe by Toe.

The value of multi-sensory learning is that the child uses his own approach to the task through using his strong areas and at the same time exercising areas of perceptual weakness. All his perceptual systems must inter-act simultaneously to make learning so secure that he can produce any aspect of the symbol when needed for reading or spelling. Wherever possible a child's individual lessons should be closely linked to his classroom language skills lesson. It can thus be seen that in an ideal situation, the child's remedial teacher is also responsible for his classroom English teaching/Numeracy and IT.

Ann Arbor Publishers produce an excellent range of resource material as well as teacher assessment tests. Some of these are listed at the end of this article.

The dyslexic child in the home

Finding a school which will both accept and tackle the problem of your dyslexic child effectively is now much easier. An organization called CReSTeD (Council for the Registration of Schools Teaching Dyslexic Pupils – www.crested.org.uk) maintains a register of schools which have had their dyslexia provision thoroughly inspected on a regular basis. There is, obviously, still the emotional impact of dyslexia on the child, and on you his parents, to consider. The dyslexic child usually knows that he has a problem when he goes to school and first attempts to read. It does not dawn on the parents until about a year later. The child does not know the name of his problem but he is aware that he is different from the other children in his class. When the teacher holds up cards with words written upon them and his peers eagerly shout out the answer, the dyslexic child sees only a jumble of symbols which are meaningless to him. Only parents who have ignored cautions about *pushing* their child will wonder before he is six why the bright inquisitive child they know at home is apparently not interested or successful in reading and other basic skills.

During this period when the child is aware and the parents are not, he feels lonely, isolated and frustrated. He is completely bewildered in the face of a strange situation. It is beyond the average six-year-old to explain to his parents his difficulties and his frustrations. He can only show his distress by his behaviour or strange quirks. Going to school is an anxiety and stomach pains, earache, headaches, or other upsets may become frequent excuses for staying at home.

A report from the British Council For Rehabilitation of the Disabled affirmed that it is rare to find a child who is not affected emotionally by years of failure in learning to read and write. The general agreement of psychiatric opinion is that when a breakdown occurs in the stages of development the likely outcome is a neurotic or behaviour disturbance. The report lists the following possible disturbances:

- The child may be aggressive or destructive;
- He may retreat into himself and become an introvert;
- He may start wetting the bed, sleep walking or develop asthma.

Dr. Macdonald Critchley in his book "The Dyslexic Child" as well as more recent research undertaken by Dr Gavin Reid in Young Offenders Institutions in Scotland shows that there is a very clear correlation between truancy and later criminality and the untreated dyslexic. The most recent study of the prison population undertaken by The Learning and Skills Council and Dyslexia Institute concludes that 52% of the prison population have literacy difficulties with the incidence of dyslexia being three to four times higher than in the general population (J.Rack 2005). It is too easy for the parent of a dyslexic child to become over-protective and stifle his development and, indeed, to neglect the needs of other children in the family. Someone once said, "You can always recognise the dyslexic child; he wears roll-neck jumpers so that he does not need to make a tie or button a shirt. He has slip-on shoes and when he puts on his coat, if he does not wear an anorak with a convenient zip, he will often button himself astray." Perhaps above all the parent must be constantly watchful and responsible. He has to walk a tightrope. He must respond to his child's predicament but must not over-protect. It is essential that the parent must not give the impression to the child that it is his very helplessness that earns his extra love. The child must know without a doubt that his parents understand the problem and mean to help him. But the object of the exercise is to make him an independent adult, not an everlastingly *difficult* child who has to be sheltered.

Ann Arbor Publishers (www.annarbor.co.uk) have produced early screening tests to identify children from as young as 4 years old who may be at risk from a dyslexic difficulty and then a full battery of diagnostic tests can be administered by a teacher who has specialised in specific learning difficulties or an Educational Psychologist. Once a positive identification has been made and a child's strengths and weaknesses have been discovered, an Individual Education Plan is prepared to provide appropriate remediation.

After reading thus far, no doubt parents and teachers will ask the inevitable question "Can a dyslexic be cured?" In answer it should be stated that since dyslexia is not an illness or disease the word 'cure' should not be used. This is because dyslexic people have a different brain structure from non-dyslexics. The right hemisphere (the creative side) of the brain is more highly developed than the left (the language side). Neurologists under Professor Albert Galaburda in the United States have now proved this having dissected donated brains from dyslexic people! Thus it can be understood that, as dyslexia is a neurological difference, it cannot be cured but if there is early identification, using different teaching techniques and strategies, the literacy difficulties can be largely overcome.

Macdonald Critchley, in his book "Dyslexia Defined", gives his "prognostic pentagon" which is made up of five favourable factors. If these factors are present there is little doubt that the dyslexic child can, in fact, largely overcome his difficulties by the time he reaches adulthood.

These five favourable factors are:

(a)   Fundamental intellectual level - it is obviously a distinct advantage for the dyslexic to be endowed with above average intellect or a high IQ.

(b)   Early diagnosis - the earlier the problem is identified the better. Any emotional problems should be evaluated and a clear distinction made between those that are primary or secondary.

(c)   A sympathetic and understanding attitude on the part of both parents and teachers. Parents must learn to come to terms with the child's difficulties in the home and teachers must have a clear understanding of the child's weaknesses in the classroom situation. Obviously this understanding on the part of teachers must extend to all who teach the child, since valuable work done by the skilled remedial teacher can be undone through a single uncharitable or uninformed remark by an unsympathetic member of staff.

(d)   The availability and the institution of intensive, skilled, sympathetic tuition - good intentions and sympathy alone are not sufficient qualifications for a remedial teacher. Experience in multi-sensory techniques and a sound knowledge of dyslexic difficulties are essential. Teaching should be done, ideally, on a one-to-one basis in short but frequent periods with constant reinforcement of skills already taught.

(e)   A powerful drive towards attainment is desirable - this can be described as guts or ego strength on the part of the child. A strong determination to succeed and overcome obstacles instead of giving up is essential for the dyslexic.

Whilst Dyslexia is now a recognised disability in the UK under both the Code of Practice (2002) and the Disability Discrimination Act (2002) there is still a lack of awareness in some areas of the country, despite the stalwart efforts of the local Dyslexia Associations.

Many of the world's greatest artists, craftsmen, architects, engineers and entrepreneurs have been, or are dyslexic. Albert Einstein, Leonardo da Vinci, Hans Christian Anderson, Richard Branson and Jackie Stewart are but a few! It is hoped that greater awareness and appropriate teaching skills will not only help dyslexic children and adults acquire vital literacy skills but will also encourage schools and parents to exploit their very many and much needed talents.

For further help :   www.bda-dyslexia.org.uk

Diagnostic Tests from Ann Arbor Publishers - www.annarbor.co.uk:

To determine those children "At Risk"
Group Screening Tests – Phillips & Leonard (Alpha, A,B,C,D, Adult depending on age)
For Full in depth Assessment
The Ann Arbor Teacher Assessment Battery (AA- TAB)
The Ann Arbor Learning Inventory (AALI)
For Reading Assessment
The Spadafore Diagnostic Reading Test (SDRT)
To Identify Reading Level (so appropriate books can be chosen)
Word Identification Scale (WIS)
To Identify Spelling Level
Quick Spelling Inventory (QSI)
To check phonic abilities and weaknesses
Phonic Based Reading Test
Quick Phonics Survey (QPS)
To Assess Visual Perception
Motor Free Visual Perception Test – Vertical MVPT-3
Test of Visual-Perceptual Skills (Non Motor) – Revised TVPS-R
Test of Visual Perceptual Skills (Non Motor) Upper Level –Revised TVPS(UL)R
Test of Visual Motor Skills – Revised (3-14 yrs) TVMS-R
To Assess Auditory –Perceptual Skills
Test of Auditory – Perceptual Skills – Revised (4-18 yrs) TAPS-3
Test of Auditory-Reasoning & Processing Skills (5 –14yrs) TARPS

Remediation Resources from Ann Arbor Publishers:

Visual Perceptual Remediation	
ALL Tracking Materials – Letter Tracking, Sentence Tracking, Word Tracking, Symbol/Letter Tracking, Music Tracking.	Eye-Hand Co-ordination Boosters
Remediation of Reversals	Perceptual Activities
ABC Mazes	The Maze Book
Classroom Visual Activities	Symbol Discrimination and Sequencing
Symbol Discrimination Series	
Auditory Perceptual Remediation	
The Listen and Learn Connection	Fine Tuning: An Auditory-Visual Training Program
Sound Out Listening Skills Program	Phonograms; for the fun of it.
Phonic Remedial Reading Lessons	
Reading Development	
High Noon Reading Scheme	High Noon Reading Comprehension
Phonics-Based Chapter Books (Key Stage 1. Interest age 7-11+)	
Spelling Development	
High Noon Spelling	
Teaching Resources	
Teaching the Dyslexic Child	Missiles to Learning
Unicorns are Real	Specific Learning Difficulties – Dyslexia
How to Write an IEP	
For Psychologists/Specialist Teachers	
WISC IV Prescriptions	WISC IV Compilation

Dyspraxia / Developmental Co-ordination Disorder

Dyspraxia followed the term *clumsy child syndrome* but now a *developmental co-ordination disorder or DCD* is the preferred term amongst professionals. It is a developmental condition which means there are factors which are evident, virtually from birth. The incidence of dyspraxia occurring with other developmental disorders (called co-morbidity) like dyslexia, attention deficit and autistic spectrum disorders is high.

There is a great overlap between the presenting symptoms of dyslexia and dyspraxia which is hardly surprising when the neurological basis for both is the same but diagnosis is dependent on which area of the brain is affected.

Dyspraxia is viewed on a spectrum and affects between 2% and 10% of the child population and between 70% to 80% are male. Despite considerable research, very little is known of the causes except that it appears to be immaturity in the area of the brain called the cerebellum. If it is not recognised that a child has dyspraxia, this can lead to secondary emotional and behavioural problems as it is easier to act the clown than it is to hide any limitations. Many dyspraxic children have average or high intelligence but then have low achievement rates in school – leading to intense frustration.

The main identifying signs are:

- Poor gross motor skills (i.e. kicking a ball, climbing, hopping and skipping).
- Poor fine motor skills (i.e. difficulties carrying out activities using the fingers – writing, tying shoelaces, doing up buttons, etc.)
- Poor Visual Perception (i.e. judging depth, judging distances, knowing their own space.) Many parents of dyspraxic children complain that when walking side by side on a pavement, the child is frequently bumping into them!
- Poor Auditory Perception (i.e. difficulties understanding instructions and being easily distracted by extraneous noises like the scraping of a chair, etc.)
- Speech Difficulties – e.g. verbal dyspraxia.

A diagnosis of dyspraxia can be made by a psychologist, occupational therapist or a physiotherapist with appropriate training. These agencies are usually accessed via a General Practitioner, Health Visitor or Paediatrician.

Dyspraxia cannot be cured because, like dyslexia, it is neurologically and not medically based but its symptoms can lessen with maturity. The prognosis is usually hopeful if an early diagnosis is made and appropriate therapy provided. This is normally occupational therapy but if speech is affected, a speech and language therapist will be involved. Many of the exercises can be done with parental involvement and, in some cases, with the co-operation and involvement of the School P.E. teacher.

In the UK, dyspraxia is regarded by the Department for Education and Skills as a disability and is included in the range of disabilities covered under the Disability Discrimination Act – Schools & Colleges, (2002).

For more information, parents should access the Dyspraxia Foundation website at www.dyspraxiafoundation.org.uk

Resources from David Fulton Publishers:

Dyspraxia – A Guide for Teachers & Parents

Resources from Ann Arbor Publishers - www.annarbor.co.uk:

Diagnostic Material for Occupational Therapists/Psychologists	
The Developmental Test of Visual Motor Integration 5th Edition VMI-5	
Quick Neurological Screening Test – 11 (QNST – 11)	
Tests of Visual-Motor Skills (TVMS –R and TVMS UL)	
Material for remediation	
Beery VMI Developmental Teaching Activities	Beery VMI My Book of Letters and Numbers
Beery VMI My Book of Shapes	Classroom Visual Activities
Revised Structured Cursive Writing	The Maze Book
Eye Hand Co-ordination Boosters	ABC Mazes

Dyscalculia
– A difficulty with numbers

Many children (and even some adults!) whilst experiencing no difficulties with reading or with the written word, have enormous difficulty understanding numbers, mathematical concepts, money, telling the time, map reading, etc. Many of those who have these difficulties have also found that, whilst they may appreciate listening to music, they are not musically inclined.

Whilst there has been a great deal of research over the last century into the causes of literacy failure, very little has been done to establish the causes of mathematical failure nor has there been any serious attempt to provide effective remedial programmes to help despite the incidence being estimated in England and elsewhere at between 3 and 6% of the school population.

The definition of dyscalculia is "an unexpected difficulty with mathematical problems". At its simplest, it is a child whose age and intellect indicate that he or she will be able to undertake a certain range of skills but who, in effect, is unable to handle maths problems that would be expected to be within his or her capacity. The Department of Education and Skills published guidance for teachers in 2001.

Some early research had suggested that dyscalculia is derived from a specific genotype – that is a genetic anomaly that may result in a specific deficit in the learning of numerical skills.

Research at University College, London suggests that dyscalculic children are troubled even by the simplest numerical tasks like selecting the larger of two numbers, counting the number of objects in a display and activating the meaning of numerals.

A recent report from the Basic Skills Agency found that poor numeracy is more of a handicap that poor literacy. In its most severe forms, children cannot learn to tell the time, know the date, shop competently nor even do simple arithmetic. There is little doubt that failure to master basic mathematics can cause intense frustration and even deviant behaviour. An inmate at one of Britain's top prisons said that he was so embarrassed by his inability to calculate money that it had been "easier to nick it than ruin his street credibility" by admitting his weakness. He went on to say that no-one had ever tried to teach him in a way that he could learn but had always shouted at him for his inability to do the simplest things.

Identifying Signs

Ask your child (or yourself) to consider the following statements:

- Sometimes I see a number written down but when I copy it, I get the numbers in the wrong order.
- I always find adding up and taking away difficult.
- I can't understand what fractions are all about.
- I could never work in a shop because I could never work out how much change to give.
- The 24 hour clock confuses me.
- I have never been able to do the times tables.
- I find it really hard to copy a stream of numbers from the board.
- Sometimes I know the answer to a maths problem but can't explain how I reached that answer.
- I am really confused between the meaning of high numbers such as 10,000 and 9,999 and I can't work out which is the higher.
- I can never work out different currency conversions.

If the majority of these statements apply to you or your child, you or they may well be dyscalculic!

For further information see www.dyscalculia.org
Information on further material written by Attwood is available from this site.

Remediation materials from Ann Arbor Publishers - www.annarbor.co.uk:

Remediation Materials
Number Tracking
Fractions
Decimals and Percentages
Cues and Signals in Math
What to do When you can't Learn the Times Tables (CD Rom) - Steve Chinn
Test of Thinking Style in Mathematics - Steve Chinn

Dysgraphia

The word *dysgraphia* simply means difficulty expressing thoughts in writing. In other words, it just means *writing difficulty*. And generally it is used to refer to extremely poor handwriting. As with dyslexia, confusion often arises when we start dealing with the term *dysgraphia* as it relates to *Special Educational Needs*. Many Local Education Authorities in the UK and in the USA do not recognise dysgraphia, in itself, as being sufficiently disabling to warrant inclusion in specialist provision.

Dysgraphia has no clearly defined criteria. A student with any degree of handwriting difficulty may be considered dysgraphic by some educational specialists. This frequently occurs when a student receives a psychological assessment outside of the state school system.

So, being labelled as dysgraphic may or may not indicate the need for specialist provision. It should be noted that most students with learning difficulties usually experience difficulty with handwriting and could probably be considered dysgraphic. However, the term is seldom used within state schools because of the lack of any strict or measurable criteria.

Underlying causes of dysgraphia:

• Sequencing (or Ordering) Problems.

As with dyslexia, written language difficulty is often believed to be the result of underlying visual or perceptual processing weakness. However, research on brain functioning has not found much evidence to support the notion of a visual basis for dysgraphia. In fact, what usually appears to be a perceptual problem (reversing letters/numbers, writing words backwards, writing letters out of order, and very sloppy handwriting) usually seems to be directly related to sequential/rational information processing. In other words, when students experience difficulty sequencing and organizing detailed information, they often have difficulty with the sequence of letters and words as they write. As a result, the student either needs to slow down in order to write correctly or experiences rather extreme difficulty with the *mechanics* of writing (spelling, punctuation, etc.). Usually they have difficulty even when they do slow down. And by slowing down or getting *stuck* with the details of writing they often lose the great thoughts that they are trying to write about. Sometimes the creative writing skills of such a student are surprisingly strong when the mechanics of writing don't get in the way. This is because their *conceptual* processing skills are often quite strong enabling them to express *deeper meaning* in spite of difficulty with the details.

Where a child under ten years is experiencing handwriting difficulties in school, a structured handwriting course is to be highly recommended. There are many excellent cursive handwriting programmes available.

For older students who still have illegible handwriting, a keyboard skills programme is to be recommended so that they can record much of their written work on a word processor thus relieving the burden on their visual/motor skills and allowing their creativity to flourish. Many public examining boards allow students to use a word processor in public examinations such as GCSE and A level if it has been recommended by an educational psychologist.

Remediation materials from Ann Arbor Publishers - www.annarbor.co.uk:

Remediation Materials
Teaching Written Expression
Springboards for Writing
Eye-Hand Co-ordination Boosters
Revised Structured Cursive Writing
Classroom Visual Activities
Perceptual Activities

Attention Deficit Hyperactivity Disorder (ADHD)

Attention Deficit Hyperactivity Disorder is the term used to describe certain behavioural problems in children. Children affected often have an unusually short attention span and become easily distracted (attention deficit), plus, they are overactive and restless (hyperactive).

Progress at school and the development of social skills may be slowed by ADHD. It can, however, be treated with behaviour modification or medication or a combination of both.

ADHD defines a type of behaviour at the extreme end of the normal range. Another term is hyperkinetic disorder. ADHD is thought to affect about 1% of the school population in the UK. The incidence in the USA is considerably higher. The incidence is four to five times more prevalent in boys than in girls. Almost all children with this disorder improve after puberty but some remain socially and educationally underdeveloped. Two thirds of children with ADHD still have some difficulties in adulthood.

There are three main types of ADHD:

- Those who are mostly impulsive and hyperactive
- Those who are mainly inattentive – known as Attention Deficit Disorder - ADD.
- A combination of the two – most commonly known as ADHD

The causes are unknown but it is believed to be genetic in origin. Children are more likely to experience ADHD if they were born prematurely, or if their mother smoked to excess and misused drugs during pregnancy. Many researchers believe that junk food, foods high in E numbers, lack of parental discipline and lack of school discipline have all contributed to the increase in ADHD and anti-social behaviour.

Whilst there are no specific tests for ADHD, checklists are used (the most common are the Connors Rating Scale and the Spadafore ADHD Checklist). For a diagnosis, the behaviour must be pervasive in two different settings (i.e. home and school). Parents who believe their child may have ADHD are advised to seek advice from a consultant paediatric psychiatrist or a consultant child psychologist.

Whilst the first avenue for treatment should be a behaviour modification programme carefully co-ordinated between home and school, the use of medication is becoming increasingly more popular with some professionals. Drugs like methylphenidate (Ritalin) and dexaphetamine originally used widely in the USA are becoming more common in Europe despite their known side effects which include dependency, weight loss, insomnia and headaches. Some of these drugs are available in slow release form giving 24 hour benefits (Concerta).

Attention to diet and the elimination of additives and caffeine in fizzy drinks as well as artificial colourings – especially in sweets is important and chocolate should be avoided. There should be greater emphasis placed on omega 3 fatty acids as found in oily fish such as mackerel, trout and herring. If a child will not eat these foods, supplements can be given instead.

Whilst the prognosis is usually good, the lack of attention and associated misbehaviour in school is bound to mean a lack of academic progress and therefore early diagnosis and treatment is vital.

More information from : www.addis.co.uk (ADHD Support Group)

Materials from David Fulton Publishers:

Attention Deficit & Hyperactivity Disorder – A Guide for Parents and Teachers

Materials from Cooper and O'Regan:

Educating Children with AD/HD – A teachers' manual

Materials from Ann Arbor Publishers - www.annarbor.co.uk:

The Spadafore ADHD Rating Scale

Aspergers Syndrome

Aspergers Syndrome is a neurobiological disorder named after a Viennese physician named Hans Asperger. In 1944 he wrote a research paper which described a pattern of behaviour found in several young boys who had normal intelligence and language development but who also exhibited mild autistic-like behaviours and with marked deficiencies in social and communication skills. It took nearly another fifty years for Aspergers Syndrome to be officially recognised as a unique disorder. In 1992 the World Health Organisation gave a diagnostic criteria for Aspergers which was separate from Autism in that language and cognitive impairments were not involved.

Aspergers is known to affect those in the average or above average ability range. The incidence ratio is 10 times greater in boys than in girls and the incidence is thought to be 36 per 10,000 (research by Gilberg 1991).

Aspergers is characterised by subtle impairments in three areas of development: social communication, social interaction and social imagination. In some cases there can be a degree of motor co-ordination and organisational problems.

The behaviour which typifies those with Aspergers must be pervasive in two different environments (i.e. home and school/work) and include the following:

- Shows a marked inability to regulate social interaction by using non-verbal language like body posture and gestures, facial expressions, eye contact.
- Does not develop peer relationships which are appropriate to developmental level.
- Does not share achievements, interests or pleasures with others.
- Lacks social or emotional awareness.
- Rigidly sticks to routines or rituals that do not appear to have a function.
- Has stereotyped repetitive mannerisms (like hand flapping).
- Has a preoccupation with parts of objects.
- Has a preoccupation with abnormal focus on a specific subject.

Associated Features:

Associated features of Aspergers Syndrome which are not required for diagnosis but are commonly present include delay in motor development – often seen as clumsiness and extreme sensitivity to sensations. In addition, many children with Aspergers will have behavioural problems due to their difficulty in understanding the world around them.

Sadly, many become the victim of bullying or teasing because of their eccentric behaviour and lack of social awareness.

Diagnosis:

Diagnosis is usually through observation by a psychologist or psychiatrist together with observational checklists completed by parents and teachers (see below).

There is no specific treatment for the disorder in itself but where the condition is co-morbid (occurring together) with other disorders like hyperactivity, obsessive compulsion, depression or anxiety, a wide variety of drug therapy is available from a General Practitioner or Psychiatrist.

When occurring alone, psychotherapy can be part of the treatment and this may include:

- Parent Education
- Behaviour Modification
- Social Skills Training
- Educational interventions.

Conclusion

One of the most disturbing aspects of Higher Functioning children with Aspergers (HFA) is their clumsy, unacceptable social skills. Though they want to be accepted by their peers, they tend to be very hurt and frustrated by their lack of social success.

Their ability to respond is confounded by the negative feedback that these children get from their painful social interactions. This greatly magnifies their social problems. When we get negative feedback, we become unhappy. This further inhibits their social skills, and a vicious circle develops.

The worse they perform socially, the more negative feedback they get, so the worse they feel and perform.

Reading Social Cues:

Though they do not appear to read social situations well, HFA children actually do. "I find I'm able to read people really well, but I usually don't respond accordingly" was the comment from one Aspergers child. Though in real time social situations, HFA's may look and feel as if they do not understand what to do. This is like the person who practises a speech until they sound like Peter O'Toole but then freeze on stage. It is not that they do not have the skills to give the speech. They have clearly demonstrated these skills and knowledge during practice. However, their emotional arousal keeps them from accessing their skills in actual situations. Most Aspergers children can explain what they need to do in social situations, thus demonstrating their knowledge; however, unlike the public speaker, they cannot demonstrate it in the real situation.

Materials from David Fulton Publishers:

An excellent book for teachers and parents is "Aspergers Syndrome – A Practical Guide for Teachers" by Cumine, Leach and Stevenson ISBN 1- 85346-499-6.

Resources from Ann Arbor Publishers - www.annarbor.co.uk:

| The Ultimate Stranger |
| You Don't Outgrow It |
| Within Reach |

A Basic Checklist for Parents and Teachers:

This is not intended as a definitive diagnostic tool but if a child scores more than 2 on many of the answers, the results need to be taken into account when a full psychological assessment is undertaken.

Please score the questions by awarding:

I if the statement is **never observed**
2 if the statement is **rarely observed**
3 if the statement is **occasionally observed**
4 if the statement is **regularly observed**
5 if the statement is **always observed**

Social and Emotional Abilities	Score
I. Does the child lack an understanding of how to play with other children? For example, unaware of the unwritten rules of social play.	
2. When free to play with other children, such as at school lunchtime, does the child avoid social contact with them? For example, finds a secluded place or goes to the library.	
3. Does the child appear unaware of social conventions or codes of conduct and make inappropriate actions and comments? For example, making a personal comment to someone but the child seems unaware how the comment could offend.	
4. Does the child lack empathy, i.e. the intuitive understanding of another person's feelings? For example, not realising an apology would help the other person feel better.	
5. Does the child seem to expect other people to know their thoughts, experiences and opinions? For example, not realising you could not know about something because you were not with the child at the time.	
6. Does the child need an excessive amount of reassurance, especially if things are changed or go wrong?	
7. Does the child lack subtlety in their expression of emotion? For example, the child shows distress or affection out of proportion to the situation.	
8. Does the child lack precision in their expression of emotion? For example, not understanding the levels of emotional expression appropriate for different people.	
9. Is the child generally uninterested in participating in competitive sports, games and other activities?	
10. Is the child indifferent to peer pressure? For example, does not follow the latest craze in toys or clothes.	

Communication Skills	Score
11. Does the child take a literal interpretation of comments? For example, is confused by phrases such as "pull your socks up, looks can kill or hop on the scales."	
12. Does the child have an unusual tone of voice? For example, the child seems to have a foreign accent or monotone that lacks emphasis on key words.	
13. When talking to the child does he or she appear uninterested in your side of the conversation? For example, not asking about or commenting on your thoughts or opinions on the topic.	
14. When in a conversation, does the child tend to use less eye contact than you would expect?	
15. Is the child's speech over-precise or pedantic? For example, talks in a formal way or like a walking dictionary.	
16. Does the child have problems repairing a conversation? For example, when the child is confused, he or she does not ask for clarification but simply switches to a familiar topic, or takes a long time to think of a reply.	
Cognitive Skills	**Score**
17. Does the child read books primarily for information, not seeming to be interested in fictional works? For example, being an avid reader of encyclopaedias and science books but not keen on adventure stories.	
18. Does the child have an exceptional long term memory for events and facts? For example, remembering the neighbour's car registration of several years ago, or clearly recalling scenes that happened many years ago.	
19. Does the child lack social imaginative play? For example, other children are not included in the child's imaginary games or the child is confused by the pretend games of other children.	
Specific Interests	**Score**
20. Is the child fascinated by a particular topic and avidly collects information or statistics on that interest? For example, the child becomes a walking encyclopaedia of knowledge on vehicles, maps or league tables.	
21. Does the child become unduly upset by changes in routine or expectation? For example, is distressed by going to school by a different route?	
22. Does the child develop elaborate routines or rituals that must be completed? For example, lining up toys before going to bed.	

Movement Skills	Score
23. Does the child have poor motor co-ordination? For example, is not skilled at catching a ball.	
24. Does the child have an odd gait when running?	
Total Number of Positive Indicators (out of 120)	

Although this is only a checklist and is not intended to provide an instant diagnosis of Aspergers Syndrome, it has been well researched and the following scores have proved useful to those professionals making a diagnosis.

Total score at 48 or below: Unlikely to have Aspergers Syndrome

Score at 49 – 72: Possibility of mild Aspergers Syndrome

Score at 73 – 96: Very likely to be Aspergers Syndrome

Score at 97 – 120: Likely to be severely affected by Aspergers Syndrome

Other Characteristics (for this section, score one if the child has shown any of the following characteristics)	Score
25. Has an unusual fear or distress due to ordinary sounds, e.g. electrical appliances.	
26. Dislikes wearing particular items of clothing.	
27. Has a fear of some unexpected noises.	
28. Dislikes seeing certain objects.	
29. Dislikes noisy, crowded places, e.g. supermarkets.	
30. Has a tendency to flap or rock when excited or distressed.	

Those children scoring 1 on Questions 25-30 will, in all probability, be those who scored between 70 and 120 on the previous questions and their answers will provide useful, additional diagnostic information.

Refer for Further Psychiatric/Psychological Examination	Yes/No

Autism

Leo Kanner's 1943 paper "Autistic Disturbances of Affective Contact" made autism a medical entity. It took twenty more years for it to be a cultural entity – intriguing to outsiders and devastating to families. Recent estimates (Bryson 1996) suggest about 1 in a 1000 children with a ratio of three or four males to each female may suffer from an Austistic Spectrum Disorder.

Autism is a brain disorder that typically affects a child's ability to communicate, form relationships with others, and respond appropriately to the environment. Some children with autism are relatively high-functioning, verbal and with an age appropriate developmental level. Others are developmentally delayed, non-verbal, or have serious language delays. For some, autism makes them seem closed off and shut down; others seem locked into repetitive behaviours and rigid patterns of thinking.

Although children with autism do not have exactly the same symptoms and deficits, they tend to share certain social, communication, motor, and sensory problems that affect their behaviour in predictable ways.

From the start, most infants are social beings. Early in life, they gaze at adults, turn toward voices, endearingly grasp a finger, and even smile.

In contrast, most children with autism seem to have tremendous difficulty learning to engage in the give-and-take of everyday human interaction. Even in the first few months of life, many do not interact and they avoid eye contact. They seem to prefer being alone, They may resist attention and affection or passively accept hugs and cuddling. Later, they seldom seek comfort or respond to anger or affection. Unlike other children, they rarely become upset when the parent leaves or show pleasure when the parent returns. Parents who looked forward to the joys of cuddling, teaching, and playing with their child may feel crushed by this lack of response.

Children with autism also take longer to learn to interpret what others are thinking and feeling. Subtle social cues-whether a smile, a wink, or a grimace may have little meaning. To a child who misses these cues, "Come here" always means the same thing, whether the speaker is smiling and extending her arms for a hug or squinting and planting her fists on her hips. Without the ability to interpret gestures and facial expressions the social world may seem bewildering.

To compound the problem, children with autism have problems seeing things from another person's perspective. Most 5-year-olds understand that other children have different information, feelings, and goals than they have. A child with autism may lack such understanding. This inability leaves them unable to predict or understand other children's reactions.

Some children with autism also tend to be physically aggressive at times, making social relationships still more difficult. Some lose control, particularly when they are in a strange or overwhelming environment, or when angry and frustrated. They are capable, at times, of breaking things, attacking others or harming themselves.

The authors acknowledge the following useful information which is from The National Autistic Society website.

Information for parents and carers. An introduction for parents and carers of people with Autism and Aspergers syndrome.

Services for parents and carers.

- N.A.S. support services: Autism Helpline; the help! programme - post-diagnostic support for parents and carers;

- Parent to Parent Line - a free, confidential telephone support service; Befriending scheme;

- The Early-Bird Programme - a training programme for parents;

- Advocacy for Education Service - advice and advocacy on special educational needs provision and entitlements for families whose children have Autism or Asperger Syndrome and conferences and events run by the NAS.

- Parent seminars and workshops—details of current courses or conferences in this subject area.

- Health professionals who are available to help—you are likely to come in contact with a number of different professionals in the course of getting a diagnosis or after you have received a diagnosis. There is a brief introduction to what each professional does.

- Ideas for family days out—being able to go out and about and enjoy the activities that all families enjoy is important for children with autism. It is also important for their siblings. There are some ideas about how to plan for activities and this service also gives details of some of the concessions that are available.

Visit The National Autistic Society at www.nas.org.uk
(The online advice and information services for parents, people with an ASD, professionals working with/for people with autism and/or their families, researchers etc. N.A.S. aim to give a response within 10 working days.)

Further help available from www.nami.org

Resources from Ann Arbor Publishers - www.annarbor.co.uk:

The Ultimate Stranger

The CHAT Test *

What is the CHAT?

CHAT stands for The CHecklist for Autism in Toddlers. It was developed by a team of researchers to help identify children who are at risk of developing social-communication disorders. It is administered by a health visitor or GP at the 18 month check up.

How is the CHAT scored?

The CHAT is very easy to score. There are 5 key items:

- A5 Pretend play
- A7 Protodeclaractive pointing
- Bii Following a point
- Biii Pretending
- Biv Producing a point

If a child fails all 5 key items, they have a high risk of developing autism. Children who fail items A7 and Biv have a medium risk of developing autism.

What happens if a child fails the CHAT?

Any child that fails the CHAT should be re-screened approximately one month later. As with any screening instrument, a second CHAT is advisable, so that those children who are just slightly delayed are given time to catch up. Any child who fails the CHAT for a second time should be referred to a specialist for diagnosis since CHAT is not a diagnostic tool.

Section A Questions for the Parent	yes/no
1. Does your child enjoy being swung, bounced on your knee, etc.?	
2. Does your child take an interest in other children?	
3. Does your child like climbing on things, such as stairs?	
4. Does your child enjoy playing peek-a-boo/ hide and seek?	
5. Does your child ever PRETEND, for example, to make a cup of tea using a toy cup and teapot, or pretend other things?	
6. Does your child ever use his/her index finger to point, to ASK for something?	
7. Does your child ever use his/her index finger to point; to indicate INTEREST in something?	
8. Can your child play properly with small toys (e.g. cars or bricks) without just mouthing, fiddling or dropping them?	
9. Does your child ever bring things to you (parent) to SHOW you something?	
Section B for a Health Professional	**yes/no**
Bii. Get the child's attention, then point across the room at an interesting object and say "Oh look! There's a {name of toy}." Watch the child's face. Does the child look across at what you are pointing at?	
Biii. Get the child's attention; then give the child a miniature tea pot and tea cup and say "Can you make a cup of tea?" Does the child pretend to pour out tea. drink it, etc?	
Biv. Say to the child "Where's the light?" or "Show me the light." Does the child POINT with his/her index finger at the light?	
Bv. Can the child build a tower of bricks? If so, how many? {Number of bricks.........}	

* acknowledgement to Paains

Obsessive Compulsive Disorder

A 10 year old girl keeps apologizing for disturbing her class. She feels that she is too restless and is clearing her throat too loudly. Her teachers are puzzled and over time become annoyed at her repeated apologies since they did not notice any sounds or movements. She is also preoccupied with *being good all the time*.

This child suffers an Obsessive-Compulsive Disorder (OCD). The National Institute of Mental Health estimates that more than 2 percent of the school population, or nearly 1 out of every 40 people, will suffer from OCD at some point in their lives. The disorder is two to three times more common than schizophrenia and bipolar disorder.

What is Obsessive-Compulsive Disorder?

Obsessions are intrusive, irrational thoughts—unwanted ideas or impulses that repeatedly well up in a person's mind. Again and again, the person experiences disturbing thoughts, such as "My hands must be contaminated; I must wash them"; "I may have left the gas stove on"; "I am going to injure myself." On one level, the sufferer knows these obsessive thoughts are irrational; however, on another level, he or she fears these thoughts might be true. Trying to avoid such thoughts creates great anxiety.

Compulsions are repetitive rituals such as handwashing, counting, checking, hoarding, or arranging. An individual repeats these actions, perhaps feeling momentary relief, but without feeling satisfaction or a sense of completion. Children with OCD feel they must perform these compulsive rituals or something bad will happen.

Most people at one time or another experience obsessive thoughts or compulsive behaviours. Obsessive-compulsive disorder occurs when an individual experiences obsessions and compulsions for more than an hour each day, in a way that interferes with his or her life.

OCD is often described as "a disease of doubt". Sufferers experience *pathological doubt* because they are unable to distinguish between what is possible, what is probable, and what is unlikely to happen.

Who gets OCD?

People from all walks of life can get OCD. It strikes people of all social and ethnic groups; and both males and females. Symptoms typically begin during childhood, the teenage years or young adulthood.

What causes OCD?

A large body of scientific evidence suggests that OCD results from a chemical imbalance in the brain. For years, mental health professionals incorrectly assumed OCD resulted from bad parenting or personality defects. This theory has been disproven over the last 20 years. OCD symptoms are not relieved by psychoanalysis or other forms of *talk therapy,* but there is evidence that behaviour therapy can be effective, alone or in combination with medication. People with OCD can often say "why" they have obsessive thoughts or why they behave compulsively. But the thoughts and the behaviour continue.

Clinical researchers have implicated certain brain regions in OCD. They have discovered a strong link between OCD and a brain chemical called serotonin. Serotonin is a neurotransmitter that helps nerve cells communicate.

In layperson's terms, something in the brain is stuck, like a broken record. Judith Rapoport, M.D., describes it in her book *The Boy Who Couldn't Stop Washing* as "grooming behaviours gone wild". OCD will not go away by itself, so it is important to seek treatment for a child. Although symptoms may become less severe from time to time, OCD is a chronic disease. Fortunately, effective treatments are available that make life with OCD much easier to manage.

What are the symptoms of OCD?

Some of the symptoms of O.C.D. are listed here. Most people don't experience all of these. You may want to say Yes or No to any symptoms you experience regularly.

What we think - Obsessions	yes/no
Fearful thoughts or pictures in your mind about being contaminated by dangerous substances, e.g. germs, dirt, AIDS.	
Frightening thoughts/images that some serious harmful events will occur because of your carelessness, for example a gas explosion in the house because the cooker is left on, that the house will be burgled because of doors or windows left unlocked or that you may have knocked someone over in your car.	
Pictures or words in your head that suggest you will harm others, especially those you care for and would never want to harm. For example that you may hurt your own child, that you may be unfaithful to your partner.	
Pictures come into your mind of your loved ones dead.	
Things in your life are not in the correct order or not symmetrical enough or in the right place, e.g. ornaments are out of alignment and you feel distressed about this.	
Blasphemous or unpleasant thoughts, pictures and doubts about your faith come into your head.	
What we do - Compulsions	**yes/no**
Check body for signs of contaminations.	
Wash, disinfect regularly.	
Avoid going to places or touching objects that you fear may contaminate you.	
Check feared situations / appliances or journey route many times.	
Avoid being the last person to leave the house.	
Avoid responsibility.	
Seek reassurances regularly from another person that everything is alright.	
Avoid situations which you feel put you at risk of harming yourself.	
Think something to yourself to "put right" the frightening thoughts – neutralising thoughts.	
Think neutralising thoughts to counteract the frightening images.	
Carry out some task which will neutralise the thought e.g. counting or saying a special word.	
Seek reassurance from others.	
You put things right or make them symmetrical many times until they "feel" right.	

What we do - Compulsions	yes/no
You avoid contact with things that make you feel like this.	
You pray, seek forgiveness frequently.	
Consult religious leader / seek reassurance.	
How do you feel when you experience some of these obsessions?	**yes/no**
Fearful	
Agitated	
Disgusted	
Guilty	
Depressed	
Tense	
Anxious	
Other................................	
How do you feel when you have carried out the compulsive behaviour or thoughts?	**yes/no**
Relieved	
Cleansed	
Calm	
Relaxed	
Less anxious	
Disappointed	
Other................................	

If you have answered YES to several of these thoughts, feelings and actions then you may have an Obsessive Compulsive Disorder.

In the last twenty years the treatment of OCD has greatly improved and most people make a good recovery. The most important treatments are cognitive (tackling the way you think) and behavioural therapy.

Medication may be prescribed by a General Practitioner or you may be offered psychiatric help. The most common medication for OCD are antidepressant drugs which can be very effective even if you are not depressed. They are non-addictive and have few side effects. They do, however, take a few weeks to work and so if you are offered this type of treatment it will be a little time until you start to feel the benefits.

The most widely accepted form of psychological treatment for OCD is Behaviour Therapy. This takes the form of a structured programme of re-education. Sufferers have to confront repeatedly what they fear (a process called *exposure*) beginning from the easiest situations and progressing through till all the feared items have been faced. At the same time the person must not perform any rituals or checks (response prevention).

It is said that up to 50% of sufferers can be helped in this way by Behavioural and Cognitive Therapists. The main goal of any therapist is to help bring about changes in the person's life which are measured and evaluated.

Goals for change may involve:

*   A way of acting
*   A way of feeling
*   A way of thinking
*   A way of dealing with physical or medical problems
*   A way of coping.

Behavioural and Cognitive Therapists can work with individuals, groups and families.

It is a sad fact, however, that OCD can easily take over people's lives and that, all too often, sufferers who do agree to therapy and then give up too early, will return to a life crippled with the illness. Many then live a life of seclusion indulging their rituals and obsessions.

Most General Practitioners, practice nurses or health visitors will be able to advise on suitably qualified cognitive & behavioural therapists in the area. There are also private clinics specialising in this field.

For further help :   www.nami.org/
Family Link : Tel :0191 2323741
NHS Direct : 0845 46 47

Materials from McGraw Hill Publishers:

Living with Fear by Isaac Marks

Materials from Fontana:

The Boy Who Wouldn't Stop Washing by Judith Rapoport

Materials from Oxford University Press:

Obsessive Compulsive Disorder – The Facts by De Silva and Rachman

Materials from Ann Arbor Publishers - www.annarbor.co.uk:

BCP Behavioural Characteristics Progression

BCP Instructional Activities

BCP Assessment Record

Moderate and Severe Learning Difficulties (MLD & SLD)

To explain fully what is meant by the educational terms *Moderate* and *Severe Learning Difficulty* it is first necessary to understand what is meant by *intelligence*.

Intelligence may be regarded as the potential ability to achieve. It is better defined by Wechsler (1944) as the "capacity of the individual to act purposefully, to think rationally, and to deal effectively with his environment." It should not be confused with the attainment which a child does in fact achieve, since laziness, illness, anxiety or a variety of other factors may be affecting the level of attainment. In general a psychologist is not concerned with measuring attainment as this is usually assessed by school tests and examinations by teachers comparing a child with his peers irrespective of potential. Intelligence consists of a general factor underpinning all purposeful thinking and behaviour together with certain specific factors. What intelligence tests measure is something important; the capacity of an individual to understand the world about them and their resourcefulness to cope with its challenges (Wechsler 1975). Intelligence is measured in terms of Intelligence Quotient (I.Q.). The national average is 100 with 34% of the population having IQs between 85 and 100 and 34% of the population having IQs between 100 and 115. This is known as the *average* range. About 16% have IQs above 115 and about 3% above 130.

The Wechsler Intelligence Scale for Children Fourth Edition (UK) is the most reliable individually administered battery of tests of cognitive abilities and its use is restricted to qualified psychologists. It is the most recent psychological instrument available (published in the UK in 2005) and is the latest in a series of Wechsler Scales which have been constantly updated, revised and re-standardised since the original, published in 1949. It assesses both verbal and non verbal ability. The tests used by teachers to measure intelligence are in fact timed verbal and non verbal reasoning tests which rely heavily on a child's levels of literacy.

Verbal items in the Wechsler Scales are all oral with no reading or writing involved. Verbal Comprehension Index measures the functioning of the left hemisphere of the brain which is the hemisphere usually responsible for speech and language whilst the Perceptual Reasoning Index measures the functioning of the right hemisphere which is usually responsible for practical, creative, artistic and visual thinking skills.

Children are described as having Moderate Learning Difficulties (or as "slow learners") if their IQ falls between 70 and 80. Statistically this accounts for 6.7% of the population. Children with Severe Learning Difficulties have IQs below 70 and account for 2.2% of the population.

The sub test scores which produce the IQ score will be uniformly depressed without the peaks and troughs which characterise a possible dyslexic profile. Both of these groups are said to have "special educational needs" and prior to the publication of the Warnock Report in 1980 and its subsequent implementation in the UK, would have been educated in special schools. The policy of *inclusion* now means that only a very hardcore of children with low levels of intellectual ability will be offered special school placement.

The implications for the curriculum and the teaching of these pupils is very different from those employed in mainstream schools and considerable repetition, patience and understanding is needed by all involved.

Further help from : www.senet.lsc.gov.uk

Resources from Ann Arbor Publishers - www.annarbor.co.uk:

Ann Arbor Teacher Assessment Battery (AA TAB)
Quick Neurological Screening Test II (QNST II)
HELP for Preschoolers Assessment Strands (3-6)
HELP for Preschoolers – Activities at Home (3-6)
Inside Help – Administration and Reference Manual for the Hawaii Early Learning Profile (birth – 3)

Giftedness

It may seem a curious anomaly that children without any apparent learning difficulty can sometimes be described as "handicapped". In many schools, however, giftedness goes unrecognised and the resulting frustration within the gifted child can easily lead to emotional and behavioural disturbance.

The question of whether we can recognize gifted children at an early age is embedded in a larger issue: how much of a child's giftedness is attributable to nature and how much to nurture? When the nature/nurture question was first raised, its author, Sir Francis Galton (1869), declared that nature was responsible for all of one's abilities. In European science and education, a backlash occurred for most of the 20th century in which nurture became the primary determinant of intelligence. Today, the pendulum has swung back to more of a middle ground and we now recognize that nature and nurture are co-parents of intelligence. Children show the signs of giftedness or advanced development early in life, but whether those gifts flower into high achievements in adult life is dependent upon the nurture they receive from their environment.

Contrary to the belief that all parents think their children are gifted, recent studies have indicated that the parents of average children do see their children's development differently from parents of gifted children. In addition, the parents of the gifted tended to underestimate their children's abilities rather than overestimate them. The two groups had similar socio-economic backgrounds and there were very few differences in physical development found between them. However, there were major differences in intellectual, imaginational and social development, as well as in talents and certain personality traits.

In a study of giftedness when parents were asked to describe their child's development over 36 months, the following interesting pattern emerged which may prove helpful to other parents who consider their child may be gifted:

Very Alert	67% Gifted	42% Average
Long Attention Span	31% Gifted	3% Average
Excellent Memory	67% Gifted	27% Average
Rapid Learner	58% Gifted	13% Average

Advanced Vocabulary	87% Gifted	34% Average
Very Observant	64% Gifted	34% Average
Very Curious	58% Gifted	40% Average
More than one imaginary friend	50% Gifted	9% Average
Vivid Imagination	46% Gifted	22% Average
High degree of creativity	66% Gifted	8% Average

One of the earliest signs of giftedness noted was alertness. A parent commented "He literally consumed his world with eagerness, wanting to learn, see, feel and touch everything, all at once."

Another early sign was long attention span. One parent commented, "He would play games longer than his playmates and get upset when they stopped playing and would leave."

Over 90 percent of the parents of the gifted saw their children as having an excellent memory. One gifted girl knew most of "Little Orphan Annie" at age two. The speed at which gifted children learned generally became apparent by the time these children were three years old. One girl could count to 20 at eighteen months of age, and could say her ABCs at age two.

It must be remembered that each gifted child is different. Certain characteristics will apply to your child and some will not. If you see that several of these characteristics fit your child, you may wish to seek further assessment of your child's capabilities so that you can nurture those abilities.

Further help from : www.gifteddevelopment.com

Resources from Ann Arbor Publishers - www.annarbor.co.uk:

Where a gifted child has been identified at an early age, reading can be a great source of information and knowledge. Many books with an appropriate reading age are, however, well below the child's interest level. The High Noon Reading Series provides excellent stimulation for such children.

Know Your Rights!

With the implementation of the Code of Practice (2002) and the Special Educational Needs Disability Act (2002) the government has placed a statutory obligation on all Local Education Authorities in England and Wales to identify and make appropriate provision for many of the disabilities described in this guide.

For those children with severe difficulties, the LEA may decide to issue a Statement of Special Educational Needs after School Action and School Action Plus procedures have been followed. The process of Statementing can be complicated and, in some cases, can prove contentious where parents and LEA disagree.

Where dialogue and recourse to a Parent Partnership Service fail to resolve the difficulties, parents have the right of appeal against the LEA's decisions through the Special Educational Needs Tribunals. This service which is totally independent but funded by the DfES is available free to parents although they will, of course, have to pay the fees of any expert witnesses which they wish to attend (i.e. independent educational psychologist, speech & language or occupational therapist).

Parents are ill advised to attend a Tribunal Hearing without legal representation and certain solicitors have gained specific experience and training in Special Educational litigation.

The Special Educational Needs and Disability Act 2001 reinforces and strengthens the original Disability Discrimination Act which was extended to schools and colleges in 2002.

It is now unlawful for schools and colleges to treat those with disabilities "less favourably" than those who are not disabled. The SENDA also recognises that many disabilities are "hidden" and are not necessarily physical.

Schools cannot discriminate for example, against dyslexic and dyspraxic pupils in their entry procedures and differentiation of the delivery of the curriculum is expected where appropriate. For example, it would be unlawful for a teacher to expect a severely dyslexic pupil with visual working memory deficits to copy laboriously from a blackboard. A hand-out of notes should be provided instead.

For many years the Joint Council for General Qualifications in England and Wales (JCGQ) which regulates GCSE and A Level examinations has agreed "special arrangements" for those who have been properly diagnosed with a disability. These not only include extra time but can include word processing, amanuensis, rest breaks and a separate room and prompter for ADHD pupils, etc.

The Scottish Qualifications Authority (SQA) goes even further and can allow a student with severe working memory deficits to have an electronic calculator in non calculator mathematics papers.

If parents think that their child is being treated *less favourably* by the school or that it is not making *reasonable adjustment* to meet his/her needs, parents should contact the Disability Rights Commission. Those with many of the difficulties detailed in this book and who are intending to study in Higher Education may be entitled to *The Disabled Students Allowance*. This allowance is intended to provide additional support, computer hardware, software etc. to aid a student with a recognised disability. In England and Wales, the Local Education Authority considers all requests but in Scotland a designated central agency deals with the DSA.

In July 2005 the DfES issued new guidelines to LEAs on the DSA. Implementation of the guidelines will be gradually introduced over the next three years. The guidelines include the format of assessments, the qualifications of the assessors, recommended tests for assessment etc.

The SpLD Working Group 2005/DfES Guidelines is available from the Department of Education and Skills or the British Dyslexia Association.

Ann Arbor resources:

> The Spadafore Diagnostic Reading Test (SDRT)
> (a DfES recommended reading test for DSA applications)

Sources of help:

Mrs M Nettleton (Solicitor)
SEN LEGAL
www.senlegal.co.uk

Independent Panel for Special Education
Advice (IPSEA)
www.ipsea.org.uk

Mr John Friel (Barrister at Law)
www.hardwickecivil.co.uk

Network 81
Tel 01279 647 415

Glossary of Terms

The following terms should be helpful to parents and teachers. There is a distinct pattern of word derivation in clinical terms relating to learning difficulties. The prefix a- usually denotes a complete or total condition, as in "agnosia" which means a complete inability to recall specific sound symbol relationships. The prefix "dys" usually denotes a partial inability, or a partial ability, to function in the area.

AGRAPHIA:
Inability to encode in written form; inability to remember how to write alphabet symbols.

ALEXIA:
Inability to decode the printed word.

ANOXIA:
Temporary loss of oxygen in important centres of the brain; usually results in brain damage which may cause learning difficulties.

APHASIA:
Inability to use language coherently or meaningfully.

AUDITORY PERCEPTION:
Difficulty in identifying ('hearing') discrete phonic elements of speech accurately; difficulty in making sound/symbol relationships.

BRADYSLEXIA:
Extremely slow rate of reading, writing or spelling.

BINOCULAR DIFFICULTIES:
A visual impairment due to the inability of the two eyes to function together.

CEREBRAL DOMINANCE:
The control of activities by the brain, with one hemisphere usually considered consistently dominant over the other. In most individuals the left hemisphere controls language function and the left is considered the dominant hemisphere.

DIRECTIONALITY:
Awareness of the vertical axis and awareness of the relative position of one side of the body versus the other.

DISCRETE:
Separate.

DISCRIMINATION:
The act of distinguishing the differences among various stimuli.

DYSFUNCTION:
Disordered or impaired functioning of bodily systems.

DYSGRAPHIA:
The inability to perform motor movements required for handwriting. The condition is often associated with a neurological dysfunction.

GESTALT:
An organised whole in which each individual part affects every other, the whole being more than the sum of its parts.

HYPERKINETIC:
Disorganised, disruptive and unpredictable behaviour, and over-reaction to stimuli usually of organic origin.

KINAESTHETIC:
Sensory modality relating to awareness of the perception of muscular effort.

LATERALITY:
Involves the awareness of the two sides of one's body and the ability to identify them as left and right correctly.

MODALITY:
The means whereby an individual receives information and thereby learns. The "modality concept" postulates that some individuals learn by one modality better than through another. For example, a child may receive and process data better through his visual modality than through his auditory modality.

PERCEPTION:
The process of organising or interpreting the raw data obtained through the senses.

PSYCHOMOTOR:
The motor effects of psychological processes and events.

SENSORY-MOTOR:
A term applied to the combination of the input of sensations and the output of motor activity. The motor activity reflects what is happening to the sensory organs such as visual, auditory, tactile and kinesthetic sensations.

VISUAL PERCEPTION:
The identification, organisation and interpretation of sensory data received by the individual through the eye.